anythink

D0622319

SHE'S GOT GAME

WOMEN IN SOFTBALL

by A.W. Buckey

FOCUS
READERS.

NAVIGATOR

WWW.FOCUSREADERS.COM

Focus Readers is distributed by North Star Editions:
sales@northstareditions.com | 888-417-0195

Produced for Focus Readers by Red Line Editorial.

Photographs ©: Sue Ogrocki/AP Images, cover, 1, 7, 9; 2nd Lieutenant Carla Stefaniak/US Air Force, 4–5; National Photo Company Collection/Library of Congress, 10–11; State Archives of Florida, Florida Memory, 13; ymgerman/iStockphoto, 15; Pxhere, 16–17; Tami Chappell/Reuters/Newscom, 19; Charlie Riedel/AP Images, 21; Warren Wimmer/Icon Sportswire, 23, 24–25; Lance Cpl. Andrew Jones/US Marine Corps, 27; Jon Osumi/Shutterstock Images, 29

Library of Congress Cataloging-in-Publication Data
Library of Congress Cataloging-in-Publication Data is available on the Library of Congress website.

ISBN
978-1-64493-063-2 (hardcover)
978-1-64493-142-4 (paperback)
978-1-64493-300-8 (ebook pdf)
978-1-64493-221-6 (hosted ebook)

Printed in the United States of America
Mankato, MN
012020

ABOUT THE AUTHOR

A.W. Buckey is a writer and pet-sitter living in Brooklyn, New York.

TABLE OF CONTENTS

CHAPTER 1

The Longest Game 5

CHAPTER 2

Early Years 11

CHAPTER 3

Olympic Dreams 17

ATHLETE BIO

Cat Osterman 22

CHAPTER 4

Softball Worldwide 25

Focus on Women in Softball • 30
Glossary • 31
To Learn More • 32
Index • 32

THE LONGEST GAME

By 11:00 p.m. on June 5, 2017, many people were asleep. But in Oklahoma City, Oklahoma, the people in the USA Softball Hall of Fame Complex were wide awake. And more than 1.5 million people were watching the softball game on TV.

Two teams were facing off in the Women's College World Series (WCWS).

The USA Softball Hall of Fame Complex began hosting the WCWS in 1990.

The Oklahoma Sooners were the previous season's champions. But the Florida Gators were the current season's top-ranked team. The two teams were locked in a tie. They had been playing for nearly five hours.

A softball game usually takes approximately two hours to play. A normal game lasts for seven innings. However, teams are sometimes tied at the end of the seventh inning. When that happens, the teams keep playing until the tie is broken.

The Sooners and Gators had reached the top of the 17th inning. The score was 4–4. The Sooners were at bat. Two

Gators player Kelly Barnhill throws a pitch during the 2017 WCWS.

Sooners had reached base. But there were also two outs. Shay Knighten stepped up to the plate. Knighten led the Sooners in runs batted in. However, she was facing Gators pitcher Kelly Barnhill.

That year, Barnhill won the ESPY Award for best female college athlete. Her 0.51 **ERA** that season was unmatched.

After three pitches, Knighten had one ball and two strikes. One more strike, and the inning would be over. On the next pitch, Knighten connected perfectly with the ball. She hit a three-run home run. The Sooners took a 7–4 lead.

In the bottom of the 17th inning, the Gators had a chance to come back. They even loaded up the bases. But the Gators only scored one more run. After their third out, the game was over. The Sooners had won the longest women's college championship game ever.

Sooners players greet Shay Knighten at home plate after her home run in the 17th inning.

The game of softball has existed for more than 100 years. People of all genders play the sport. However, most college and professional softball players are women. Women's softball is an exciting, always-changing game.

CHAPTER 2

EARLY YEARS

Softball was invented in a single afternoon. On Thanksgiving in 1887, a group of men started to play ball. They used a boxing glove and broom handle. The ball game the men played was a lot like baseball. However, they used a larger ball and played inside. Over time, people started playing this new game outside.

A woman pitches during a softball game in the early 1900s.

By 1923, the game had official rules. By the late 1920s, it was named softball.

Softballs are larger than baseballs. But softball fields are smaller than baseball fields. Softball games last seven innings, while baseball games last nine.

Women played both baseball and softball in the 1800s and 1900s. In the 1900s, some women played professionally. During World War II (1939–1945), many male baseball players fought for the US military. In response, some businesspeople decided to form a women's league.

The All-American Girls Softball League started playing in 1943. Later,

Dottie Schroeder swings during a 1948 game in the All-American Girls Baseball League.

the league's name changed to the All-American Girls Baseball League. In fact, the games in this league were somewhere between baseball and softball. Players used mostly baseball rules on a softball field. Dottie Schroeder was one of the league's best players. Schroeder was a shortstop with a strong arm. She started in the league when she was only 14 years old.

The All-American Girls Baseball League was popular in the 1940s. However, it became less popular after World War II ended and men returned home. It went out of business by 1954. Schroeder was the league's only player to play in every season.

SLOW-PITCH AND FAST-PITCH

For the 1965 World Championship, teams played fast-pitch softball. In this type of softball, the pitcher winds her arm around to pitch the ball. This motion allows for greater pitch speed. Another type is slow-pitch softball. In slow-pitch, the pitcher cannot wind up her arm. Both types of the game have been played for many decades.

The 1965 Women's Softball World Championship took place in Melbourne, Australia.

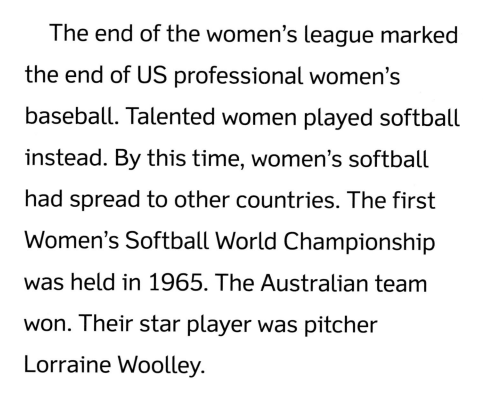

The end of the women's league marked the end of US professional women's baseball. Talented women played softball instead. By this time, women's softball had spread to other countries. The first Women's Softball World Championship was held in 1965. The Australian team won. Their star player was pitcher Lorraine Woolley.

CHAPTER 3

OLYMPIC DREAMS

Through the 1970s, women's softball continued to grow. In 1972, a law called Title IX helped the sport grow even more in the United States. This law required schools to give female and male athletes **proportional** funding. As a result, many US colleges began offering athletic **scholarships** to women.

After Title IX, both college and high school softball participation increased.

These scholarships supported a new generation of softball players. Dot Richardson was one of these players. In 1979, Richardson attended Western Illinois on a full athletic scholarship. After one year, she switched to the University of California, Los Angeles. During college, she was an All-American four times.

Richardson also played for Team USA during the 1996 Olympics. That year was softball's first time at the Games. Richardson helped the United States win gold in 1996 and 2000. Crystl Bustos was another star on the 2000 US team. Bustos was a **designated player** and a power hitter. With her on the team, the

Crystl Bustos homers during the 2004 Olympic Games.

United States won a third straight gold in 2004.

Women's softball appeared to be reaching new heights. In 2004, a US professional softball league started. The league was called National Pro Fastpitch (NPF). In 2005, the first-ever World Cup of Softball was held. Japan won the championship.

At the same time, the **International** Olympic Committee (IOC) worried that softball was too much of a US sport. In 2005, the IOC decided to take softball out of the 2012 Olympics. Many players were disappointed by the news.

Even so, the 2008 Olympics proved to be the most exciting yet. The United

YUKIKO UENO

Yukiko Ueno was one of the first softball players to pitch faster than 70 miles per hour (113 km/h). Ueno is also known for her **endurance**. During the 2008 Olympics, Ueno threw 413 pitches in three games over two days. Many fans agree that Ueno is one of the best softball players of all time.

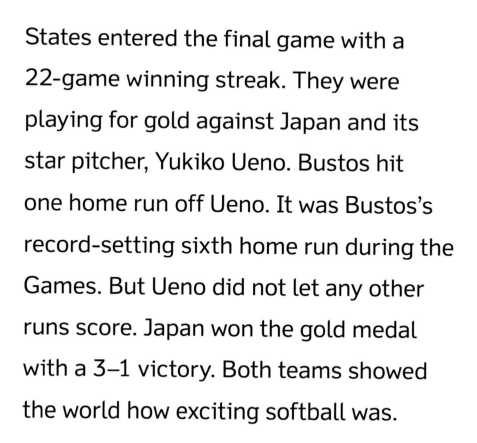

Yukiko Ueno winds up to pitch during the 2008 Olympic Games.

States entered the final game with a 22-game winning streak. They were playing for gold against Japan and its star pitcher, Yukiko Ueno. Bustos hit one home run off Ueno. It was Bustos's record-setting sixth home run during the Games. But Ueno did not let any other runs score. Japan won the gold medal with a 3–1 victory. Both teams showed the world how exciting softball was.

CAT OSTERMAN

Cat Osterman was born in 1983 in Houston, Texas. Osterman was a star softball player at the University of Texas. In college, she played three times in the College World Series. She also threw 20 **no-hitters** and 9 **perfect games**.

After college, Osterman became a pro softball player. She pitched for the US national team from 2001 to 2010. She helped that team win Olympic gold in 2004 and silver in 2008. On Team USA, Osterman had an incredible 0.38 ERA. She also averaged nearly two strikeouts per inning.

In 2015, Osterman retired from softball. However, she missed playing the game. Then she learned softball was returning to the Olympics in 2020. So, in 2019, Osterman rejoined the US national team.

Cat Osterman stares down a batter during a National Pro Fastpitch game in 2012.

CHAPTER 4

SOFTBALL WORLDWIDE

Women keep pushing softball to new levels. For example, in 2012, Monica Abbott pitched a record-setting 77 miles per hour (124 km/h). She also became one of the best pitchers in the NPF. Between 2006 and 2017, she had a career ERA of 1.04. During that time, she helped win five NPF championships.

Monica Abbott pitches for the Chicago Bandits during a 2012 NPF championship game.

Softball has continued to become more international. Since 2017, the NPF has added three teams from outside the United States. These teams are from China, Australia, and Canada.

In addition, many US players have joined leagues outside the United States. For instance, Abbott began playing in the Japan Women's Softball League (JWSL) in 2009. This league has been active since 1968. In 2018, Abbott helped the Toyota Red Terriers win the championship.

In 2018, the IOC made another announcement. Softball was coming back to the 2020 Olympics. In 2018, 67 countries around the world had ranked

In July 2018, the US national team played the Toyota Red Terriers of the JWSL.

national softball teams. But only six of those teams could go to the Olympics. To qualify, teams had to perform well in certain international games.

However, in 2019, the IOC decided to take softball out of the 2024 Olympics.

This decision set back the sport again. Without a place in the Olympics, teams often struggle to find funding. As a result, it can be hard to support new talent.

Still, softball remains popular. In 2017, nearly 300 US Division I colleges fielded

JANET LEUNG

Between 2016 and 2018, Canada's softball team was ranked third in the world. Janet Leung helped keep the team near the top. Leung was born in Mississauga, Ontario. She played college softball at Brown University in the United States. She was one of the school's best hitters. In 2017, she started playing with the Canadian national team. She has excelled as the team's shortstop. In 2018, she helped her team win the Canada Cup.

In 2018, softball was the fifth-most popular sport for high school girls.

softball teams. That same year, more than 365,000 girls played high school softball in the United States. And many countries, such as Mexico and China, have improved their national teams. Despite setbacks, new women's softball champions will continue to shine around the world.

FOCUS ON
WOMEN IN SOFTBALL

Write your answers on a separate piece of paper.

1. Write a sentence that describes the key ideas from Chapter 3.

2. Which women's softball player would you most like to watch? Why?

3. What position is Yukiko Ueno known for?

    A. shortstop
    B. designated player
    C. pitcher

4. Why might Monica Abbott's pitch speed help her be such a great pitcher?

    A. Batters have less time to react and swing.
    B. Batters cannot hit pitches at certain speeds.
    C. Pitching fast helps Abbott aim.

Answer key on page 32.

GLOSSARY

designated player
A player who mainly bats and plays limited defense.

endurance
The ability to keep doing something for a long time.

ERA
Short for earned run average. In softball, this statistic is the average number of runs that a pitcher gives up every seven innings.

international
Having to do with many different countries.

no-hitters
Games in which a pitcher does not allow any hits.

perfect games
Games in which a pitcher does not allow any players on base.

proportional
Having numbers or amounts that have the same relationship between one another.

scholarships
Money given to students to pay for education expenses.

TO LEARN MORE

BOOKS

Axon, Rachel. *Title IX Levels the Playing Field*. Minneapolis: Abdo Publishing, 2018.

McIntyre, Abigael, and Ann Wesley. *Fast-Pitch Softball: Girls Rocking It*. New York: Rosen Publishing, 2016.

Rissman, Rebecca. *Top Softball Tips*. North Mankato, MN: Capstone Press, 2017.

NOTE TO EDUCATORS

Visit **www.focusreaders.com** to find lesson plans, activities, links, and other resources related to this title.

INDEX

Abbott, Monica, 25–26
All-American Girls Baseball League, 13–14

Barnhill, Kelly, 7–8
Bustos, Crystl, 18, 21

ERA, 8, 22, 25

International Olympic Committee (IOC), 20, 26–27

Japan Women's Softball League (JWSL), 26

Knighten, Shay, 7–8

Leung, Janet, 28

National Pro Fastpitch (NPF), 19, 25–26

Olympics, 18, 20, 22, 26–28
Osterman, Cat, 22

Richardson, Dot, 18

Schroeder, Dottie, 13–14

Ueno, Yukiko, 20–21

Women's College World Series (WCWS), 5
Women's Softball World Championship, 14–15
Woolley, Lorraine, 15

Answer Key: 1. Answers will vary; **2.** Answers will vary; **3.** C; **4.** A